Copyright © 2021 Tekkan
Artwork Copyright © 2021

All rights reserved.
First Printing, 2021
ISBN 978-1-7363537-6-9

To contact Tekkan please email:
buddhaboy1289@gmail.com

Table of Contents

Things that Happened at
the Poetry Workshop . . . . Page 95

How to Read My Poems

I want to be direct in my meaning — I want people to clearly understand my meaning. My wordiness is inspired by Shakespeare, and the (aimed-for) concision is in imitation of Japanese style. Using the sonnet with the tanka, I mix the sensibility of the Occident and the Orient — which I have done by living in England, Japan, and America.

I have married the sonnet to the tanka. Often, I don't rhyme my sonnets, because I want freer expression. I tell a story in the sonnet — using three quatrains separated by line spaces, and a final couplet. The story builds to a conclusion in the couplet. The tanka is a commentary, or a counterpoint, to the sonnet — the combined poems have two endings.

Recently I have added limericks, doggerel, and rhymed sonnets into my repertoire. The limericks have a rhyme scheme but the tanka do not.

I don't punctuate much in my poetry. I want the words themselves to do the work. There is logic between words, and the forms provide structure. By not using punctuation I hope to direct readers to carefully attend to each word — to appreciate the graininess of words.

Reading my poems silently and reading them aloud may be different experiences. When I'm not rhyming my sonnets, there's not always a pause intended at the end of the line.

Hint: *unrhymed sonnets are to be recited not as lines but as phrases, and a phrase often overflows the break at the end of a line. I pause and take a breath where it seems natural for me to pause. Another person may pause differently than I do.*

Each poem is a piece of a mosaic, and it is my hope that the collection of poems forms an accurate portrait of consciousness.

My friend, *Will Ersland*, is a wonderful artist. His artwork graces the cover of this book. My daughter Jocelyn Suzuka Figueroa painted the hummingbird and the sunburst.

I am Barry MacDonald. I received the *dharma* name *Tekkan*, which means "Iron Man," a settled practitioner of great determination.

— *Tekkan*

Everyday Mind XXIII

Humidity
and heat make my
skin sticky with
sweat — the sun is
orange.

The Buddha is said to have remembered
All of his past lives including when he
Was a dolphin which must have reappeared
To him perhaps as one of his happy
Incarnations while I can't see beyond
The boundaries of this apprehensive
Human being which to me is a bond
That is sometimes hard involving pensive
Episodes and I am imagining
What life would be like if I were a stag
Living under the sun and moon roaming
Amid the woods and fields without a lag
Between my sensations and perceptions
With much less complicated decisions.

I am sure there would
be competition with the
other stags over
does but there would also be
much frolic in my swiftness.

The humidity is evident as
Soon as I rise from bed and the air
Is cool early in the morning and has
A tangible liquid quality compared
To what it is in the depth of winter
When I am compelled to use lip balm to
Keep my lips from cracking and it's better
To spread lotion on my skin as I do
To prevent my skin from itching so I
Really do love summer when I may lounge
About the house with all the windows wide
Open without the hinderance to scrounge
For a few moments of natural warmth
Which is a benefit of summer's worth.

By about the mid-
point of afternoon the heat
will begin to sear
the moisture in the air and
everything begins to cook.

Day after day the sun in the summer
Often appears by itself in the sky
And its corona is a bright glimmer
Of white-hot heat which makes everything dry
Despite the humidity — if there are
Many days without the refreshment of
Rain then the yards of grass do become charred
Which is a part of summer I don't love
And last night the sky was cracking with peals
Of thunder and flashing with lightning bolts
Which made the phenomenal sky surreal
Dimming and lighting with electric volts
But today there's no evidence about
Of any rain and we are in a drought.

A couple of days
ago the sunset was a
brilliant orange as
a result of the wildfires
combusting in Canada.

Because I am a sincere person who
Usually does do the right thing and
I may slip into self-righteousness too
I do make a lot of mistakes offhand
And later on I think about what I
Did and I'm excessively critical
Of myself thinking I am a bad guy
Not wanting to be hypocritical
Then I'm looking in a funhouse mirror
And all my features and behaviors are
Distorted and my self-image shimmers
Which is a state that is very bizarre
And then I know there's something I should do —
I had better relax — or I am blue.

It's much easier
to do what I gotta do
while forgetting my
self-image which is not
something that's easy to do.

I share my house with a liberated
Being whom I have named Kitcat and he
On occasion can be frustrated
But he is happy ordinarily
His motivations aren't calculated
He thinks and acts instantaneously
Some of the time he is animated
For the bulk of the day he is sleepy
He certainly can be agitated
But I never doubt his sincerity
He's not in the least bit fabricated
He flows with a blissful simplicity
I don't think he's ever been dejected
He's much more likely to be elated.

For some reason he
will suddenly scamper
through the house as fast
as he can without ever
asking for permission first.

I have an uneasy relationship
With the system governing the nation
As our rulers do resort to their whips
To compel behavior to their notions
Which revolve around dividing people
Into perpetrators and rescuers
And victims using a trick that appeals
To our self-pity which is quite sincere
And the trick works because of the use of
Malefactors who need to be defeated
Which rescuers do because of their love
And the agitation is repeated
Ceaselessly because it is so easy
To play the victim and to be lazy.

What would people do
if they realized
they are playing each
of the roles in turn?

Perhaps it's obvious that any way
Of governing a mass of people will
Involve tricks and coercion to convey
Some peace hopefully without overkill
But this is a human predicament
To which I'd rather not devote too much
Thought as I don't want to become hellbent
On winning the argument inasmuch
As squabbling and suffering doesn't
Ever end and I'd rather find my peace
In sincere companionship that isn't
Based on leverage but that brings release
In the awareness and acceptance of
My craziness — as I'm looking for love.

I do need friends who
can occasionally put
disagreements out
of mind as opinions are
needlessly combustible.

She is my maybe lover who wants to
Talk to me on the phone every morning
At 5 a.m. which I've fallen into
Because I think that I may be getting
Somewhere with her but I'm not at all sure
Because at times she will disappear and
And then I am crestfallen and unsure
That we'll ever talk again and I'm stunned
When she comes back into my life again
With a flimsy excuse usually
Having to do with her divorce that strains
Credulity but she talks beautifully
And she has a way of hooking me that
Works — I don't know what to do about that.

I've convinced
myself our talking at
odd hours is harmless
and inconsequential.

I am not without my defenses as
I'm relying on my meditation
And deploying nonchalance with the jazz
Engaging in bantering flirtation
And if you could see me lying in bed
As I am speaking to her you would see
A guy in his element spouting threads
Of ebullient curiosity
Dissecting the absurdities of our
Society and yes I am talking to
Her deep in conversation for an hour
But I could speak to anyone and do
The same as I am a guy who is free
And as casual as I want to be.

And yet she could go away
And I wouldn't get my way
And that would be bad
And I would be sad
But really what can I say?

As I ride my bicycle down a length
Of mostly unused asphalt road every
Afternoon pedaling in the wavelength
Of the summer sun which can be hazy
I can see dozens of grasshoppers on
The road and they are startled by my bike
And they are a surprise to come upon
As everyone will jump and some will strike
Me as I'm passing by and they don't hurt
And I find the phenomenon funny
Which I can't do anything to avert
In summer on asphalt when it's sunny
As this is the season for grasshoppers
In autumn — woolly bear caterpillars

In autumn woolly
bear caterpillars on the
asphalt undulate
across and along my way
but they don't see me at all.

Summer is the time for being lazy
So this poem won't be important and
I can't focus when the air is hazy
So I might as well be sleepy and bland
And write about nothing which is not as
Easy as it might seem as I do need
To be sufficiently careful whereas
If I weren't no one would bother to read
These words and that would be a blow to my
Ego and so today I will confess to you
That for years I've been intending to buy
A hummingbird feeder which I would do
For entertainment but I am lazy
Especially when the air is hazy.

It's so simple to
put up a feeder to see
the hummingbirds but
I haven't got around to
doing it as of today.

As I'm lying awake in bed idly
Waiting for 5 a.m. I can listen
Half-heartedly lackadaisically
To the distant hum of the traffic when
I discover the birds have stopped singing
As they did in spring and I guess they are
Done with mating and summer is bringing
An absence I haven't noticed before
So I keep myself occupied looking
At the clock and listening to the sounds
Of people moving about and driving
Wherever they are going around town
And doing whatever it is they do
Generating an echo as they go.

I'm just waiting for
the clock to get to
5 a.m. when I'll call
and hear her say my name
again and then we'll converse.

I am not as captivated as I
Was and I am practicing nonchalance
With a better estimation of why
We are talking so much in response
To an emptiness and seeing what can
Be done with words at an odd hour of
The day which is perhaps better now than
Not talking in imitation of love
With lighthearted exploration minus
Any expectations of entangled
Consequences as our chat is about
Cavorting with innovative angles
Making a festival of all of our doubts
So we are playing with patterns of words
And being serious would be absurd.

However much we
affect each other I am
able to attend
to my livelihood without
bewildering illusions.

When rushing on the highway it's common
To see the fields of corn or soybeans in
August but today I saw the awesome
Sight of a field of sunflowers wherein
A multitude of yellow faces piqued
My interest with their curious stance
Blossoming at the peak of summer heat
Which I appreciated in a glance
As a blandishment of summer with a
Blazing sun hanging in the sky keeping
Steady pace with my speeding car with the
Army of yellow faces emerging
And vanishing while bringing a smile to
My face which is a lovely thing to do.

Without a word the
sunflowers in serried ranks
gaze patiently up
at the exuberance of
the vibrant summer sunshine.

Please indulge me as I engage my wit
Gathering a ridiculous group of
Words which may in fact entirely fit
Wherein each line follows the one above
Weaving with a semblance of logic which
Gives the impression of progress to a
Satisfying conclusion with a pitch
Inciting curiosity in the
Meaning of words and the significance
Of the ceaseless parading of events
Which is important that it does make sense
Otherwise it wouldn't be worth a cent
As there is a worthiness in spinning puns
Anticipating the punchline is fun.

Can there be sincerity
Coupled with veracity
Pulling you along
With a little song
Leading to serenity?

I need to find a posture that helps to
Keep me balanced and happy even when
I lose a friend and don't know what to do
Because I know the value of a friend
So with an end of communication
Without a reason I can understand
I do feel a familiar frustration
In a feeling of isolation and
I don't believe it's helpful to evade
A sense of loss or to engage in a
Fit of anger or to become afraid
That somehow I am unworthy of the
Solicitude of a friend and so then
I can boomerang and begin again.

I don't believe that
I'm the only one who has
accumulating
grief that disguises itself
under other emotions.

This is the tipping point of the year when
The air in the morning is cool and comes
In through my open windows and yet then
The afternoons are sweltering on some
Days and the heat is beastly which isn't
A condition a person enjoys but
Unconsciously adapts to and doesn't
Notice or bellyache about but what
Does get to me is when I drive about
Town and I can see in scattered patches
The first touches of autumn leaves without
A doubt and every year the sight catches
Me because it points in the direction
Of February and disaffection.

I suffer from a
syndrome called
post-traumatic
February disorder
and can't be talked
out of it.

I am trudging on the road to happy
Destiny putting my faith in a net
Of ancient ideas that I believe
And without knowing what I'm doing yet
I am following the resonance of
My heart which says that each of us is an
Imperishable imbecile of love
Beyond knowing how the journey began
And hemmed about with a forgetfulness
Doing my wholehearted best on this day
And flirting with liberation I guess
But when it is coming I cannot say
Recalling a message that it's easy
Like relaxing within a peaceful breeze.

The way is easy
as long as I do my best
and not worry at
all about the outcome of
everything that I may do.

She likes to go to garage sales and I
Went along with her in the afternoon
And we explored the rolling countryside
As I wanted the chance to be in tune
With her with the casual passage of
Time within the close confines of a car
Even though I really don't share her love
For buying things — we did find a bazaar
Where I bought a pair of cowboy boots and
I don't remember what she got as I
Just wanted to be with her somewhat stunned
When she suddenly wanted to drive by
All the bars where her ex-husband drinks to
See if he was inside and drinking too.

She had me driving
to places I had never
been to and wouldn't
ever return to as I
explored her quirky habits.

Her not being able to let go of
Where her ex-husband is or what he may
Be doing is a signal to me of
A crazy fixation as much to say
That she's obsessed with him and can't let go
Which means that she's thinking more about him
Than me which I've suspected even though
She is with me now the chances are slim
That I'll be the guy she's dreaming about
Especially while she's consumed with her
Failed marriage even though he's a lout
So I'm beginning to think she prefers
Abuse mixed in with excitement perhaps
Which I think clearly leads to a collapse.

Presently she is
like a loaf of half-baked bread
and the yeast has to
be left alone to do its work
before there can be flavor.

What am I going to do now that I can
See that I am not the center of her
Attention and I need to have a plan
That's sensibly based on what I prefer
Because I like her company and as
I am engaged in a fantasy of
Possessing her — so should I quit? Whereas
I love the feeling of being in love
And maybe we can keep talking without
Doing any harm to each other or
Mostly to me if I can figure out
How to hang in there and open the door
To the possibility of love — or
To keep her from becoming a big chore?

There is curiosity
Inside our verbosity
Involving some clues
Of what we could do
With some reciprocity.

This is a quiet thunder rumbling from
A distance and it has soft edges and
A gentle touch not like a booming drum
And not like the sudden claps and cracks and
The tearing of the sky that I have heard
But instead it is so grand and wondrous
Which is difficult to put into words
When definitions are superfluous
And this thunder does mean something to me
As it reveals an echoing vastness
Of horizons I'm not able to see
Of mysteries concealed by the darkness —
This thunder is casting a soothing spell
It is a summons like a temple bell.

Also the patter
of continuing rain has
a gentle cadence
coming through open windows
carried along in a breeze.

My experience now is to watch the
Ups and downs of my daily life and to
Know when I'm not at my best and that a
New circumstance is arriving to do
Whatever it will to change my mood and
I realize that I can't wrench myself
Into a better mood but that I can
Learn to surf emotions as life itself
Is a continuing vibration of
Ups and downs much like the crests and the troughs
Of waves and I will weather my share of
Disappointment and success and slough off
The weight of serious expectations
And learn to live with my fluctuations.

It's easy to talk
this way but there's a trick in
really living this
way which involves letting go
of serious assumptions.

This habit I have of writing sonnets
Is kind of crazy and doesn't make sense
As I can't see that I'll ever profit
Financially and I have no pretense
Of doing more than just playing with words
Putting them together in odd ways and
Deploying irony may be absurd
Upsetting expectations if I can
By relying on my sincerity
Traipsing in a definite direction
Practicing my verbal dexterity
Not caring about remuneration
Because — as much as you — I want to see
What this crazy poem is going to be.

Don't ask me how this
poem is going to finish
because I haven't
a clue until I blunder
on a happy finale.

The birds are not as noisy as they were
During their springtime exuberance as
The mating season is done and they are
Liberated now and have much less sass
About defending their territory
But they can be heard now and again as
In sporadic joyful oratory
And they do lighten my heart as I pass
Setting me free from the clutch of my thoughts
And the birds are often invisible
Hidden in foliage but I can spot
Them in the air when I'm able
To absorb myself in my surroundings
And attending to birds is a wingding.

Foliage hides
the absolutely
unique twisting
of each branch.

I'm not liberated because I'm still
Engaged in pursuit of this woman who
Knows very well that I'm obsessed and will
Call her every morning and join her too
At least once a week for lunch or supper
In restaurants or cafés and a day
Ago I drove her to a carpet store
As I'm doing my best to find a way
To insinuate my presence into
Her life and it's all very well for the
Buddha to be autonomous and to
Not be concerned about results in a
Meditative state of serenity
But I do want her reciprocity.

She says she talks to
me more than to anyone
else in her life and
that's the sort of comment that
keeps me so interested.

The other day she recruited me with
Several other big guys to move her
Oak armoire which was such a heavy lift
Out of her ex's house and up the stairs
To her townhouse and I was the guy on
The left front of it and to pull it up
To strain my back and legs to come upon
One more step above without giving up
And in between each heave its weight would drop
With a prodigious thud and it almost
Smashed my foot but we made it to the top
After I had expended my utmost
Energy and I am glad that it is done
Because there are other ways to have fun.

The ordeal was
another way for me to
ingratiate my
potency into her good
graces — at least I hope so.

It's a question when I'm assembling
Words whether I'm giving preference to
My ears or eyes as I will be saying
Words over again and listening to
The way they tickle my ears and also
I will be counting syllables to put
A pleasing number within each line so
I can measure every metrical foot
And I will be taking the time to rhyme
Coming at the end of every line but
It is not my habit at every time
To be obvious and so to see what
I am doing you have to read the words
To discover whether they are absurd.

If there isn't a
sufficiently pleasing thread
of meaning to keep
you following me you would
stop listening or reading.

I've got to carry on with this girl and
Not give a damn whether what I want comes
About or not as I do what I can
And am learning at least a little some
Of the ploys involved in being relaxed
And passionate at the same time and how
I can do that and not become attached
To the results is a trick that somehow
Comes along perhaps only through doing
Exactly what I'm doing and it might
Be more propitious to be taking
More time to see whether she is the right
One for me as there are indications
That she likes to perpetrate frustrations.

Being together
doesn't necessarily
mean that we are
getting somewhere or
will arrive together.

I'm ashamed to be laughing at people
By looking at a website that shows their
Hideous tattoos like the fellow who
Emblazoned the words "No Regerts" on his

Arm as a determined declaration
Of stupidity or the guy who sports
A frightening black widow spider that
Covers a quarter of his face or the

Sad and monstrous depictions due to
The incompetence of the artist of
A parent's daughter or son as I can
Imagine the weight of embarrassment

And horror and regret on the morning
Afterward that surely must come to them.

Scrolling through dozens
of photos of hideous
tattoos inspires
fascination similar
to a traffic accident.

Kitcat manages to express himself
Very well without the benefit of
Words as he employs a variation
Of yowls with the tenor of a rising

Or a descending quality and he
May on occasion be monotone but
He is sure to moderate the length of
His utterance and there's a difference

Of emphasis along a spectrum from
Quiescence to mildly interested
To insistence to excited and to
Absolute vehemence as when I tread

On his tail that elicits from me my
Most abashed and heartfelt apology.

When he wants a treat
he knocks the container off
of the counter and
expresses a simple yowl that
cannot be misunderstood.

Ours is a culture of videos and
Press releases and of the branding and
The endorsement of celebrity
Products and of accepted opinions

Perpetuating associations
Of inclusion or exclusion and our
Hearts are burdened with the task of
Finding where and with whom we will find home

Amid the susceptibility of
Human fallibility and I would
Like to transform resentments into
The acknowledgment of hurts whereby

I no longer need to blame anyone
Which to me would be a liberation.

I would like to be
as light as a feather with
as many people
as possible while choosing
my skirmishes carefully.

What I take from the Bhagavad Gita
Is the direction to be wholehearted
While letting go of results which is a
Trick when I'm in a pattern of waking

In the night with energized thoughts that are
Heavy with misapprehensions about
The people I know whom I'm not getting
Along with as well as I would like to

Arousing me from my bed to fold my
Legs and meditate in the darkness to
See what may be accomplished with a
Posture of tension counterbalanced with

A relaxation of consciousness that
Allows for the relinquishing of thoughts.

The tension of the
spine and the relaxation
of the shoulders make
for the combustion of an
energy that burns my thoughts.

I was pedaling in ignorance up
The hills and along the long stretches of
The countryside and comparing myself
To the reported average speed of

The riders of the *Tour de France* mindful
Of what a laggard I would appear next
To they who have transformed the muscles of
Their bodies into a sleek resemblance

Of the tubular composition of
Their bicycles apart from their hefty
Thighs and calves that pump incessantly with
Enviable speed leaving me behind

While I was ignorantly working so
Much harder than was necessary.

I had only to
pump air into the tires
to reach the proper
pounds per square inch and then I
could race like a maniac

Whether I should gamble and go to my
45th high school reunion was the
Question at the bowling alley and bar
Because at the 40th I learned that

Most of the group were strangers to me and
Our talking was an awkward groping for
Connections that couldn't be founded on
The past because I couldn't recall it

But on the other hand I've traveled to
Several nations and I have stories
To tell and I could start a new friendship
And I haven't been pummeled nearly as

Much with the ugly stick as the others
Have and I could have a romantic fling.

At the 40th
an enthusiastic and
inebriated
fellow bellowed my name but
who he was I couldn't say.

I found a white feather on the grass by
The river and the shaft is thick at its
Base and narrows as it goes along and
Is pointedly thin at the feather's end

And the shaft is weightlessly hollow — while
The vane of the feather is translucent
And on one side the vane is narrow and
Has a straight edge but on the other it's

Wide and curves in a graceful line — and when
I swish the feather up and down beside
My cheek as if it were a Japanese
Fan I can feel a wafting of the air

And maybe the feather came from a gull
Or it might have been left by a pigeon.

From now on I will
wear the feather inside the
band of my straw hat
as an epitome of
a natural jewelry.

I keep a marble urn on top of a
Chest of drawers in my bedroom and in the
Urn there are a dozen peacock feathers and
And the urn itself is sandy colored

And speckled with pink and red rosettes and
The peacock feathers are explosions of
Frilly extravagance and these things have
Been inside my room for decades and I

Don't think about them very much but
When I do I see the manmade shape of the
The urn that shows the hidden beauty of
The earth and I notice the feathers that

Are bright exotica of a bird that
Also has an origin like the earth.

The feathers and the
urn are like bookends
of phenomena that
arose from emptiness.

The ancient Bhagavad Gita concerns
Itself with subtleties of nature and
Of consciousness consoling me with a
Pronouncement beyond my understanding

Saying that consciousness continues through
Lifetimes bordered by a forgetfulness
That prevents me from becoming weary
And disheartened with poignant memories

So that the imperishable game of
Life is fresh in the moment and I may
Act spontaneously without worry
Of losing my chances forever as

I am free to experience loss and
Suffer and triumph again and again.

The thing to do is to
act wholeheartedly
without worry
about results.

I enjoyed my high school reunion
Last night a little ashamed that classmates
Remembered me much better than I did
With them but the more we talked the more I

Recognized and the evening presented
A sweet poignancy in the person of
Heidi Junker who rode on the school bus
With me on whom I had a crush but I

Was too shy to summon my impulses
To fruition and Heidi was surprised
And amused by my confession saying
She would have dated me as she sadly

Thought that because her dad was the quirky
Mayor she lost many chances for dates.

I remember her
as bespeckled and cute with
such pleasing curves
that inspired sensuous
and curious impulses.

Jim Morton found me again on Facebook
And we shared our memories on the phone
Of living in Kyoto Japan 30
Years ago and we reminisced about

Teaching English to the Japanese and
About being able to escape and
Go to *Hoshinnji* where the Zen master
Harada would hold practice periods

Of silent meditation in pursuit
Of the *Dharma* in the sincere manner
Of any of the ancient masters from
Hundreds of years ago in China or

Japan because that is how *Dharma*
Is transmitted — from master to student.

Harada filled my
abdomen with a glowing
warmth during our last
private interview showing
me true generosity.

I met Jim through a teaching buddy and
I drove a scooter to his home after
My evening lessons and we would sit in
Meditation and lift heavy barbells

And he introduced me to *Hoshinnji*
And he became my bridge to the *Dharma*
And he opened a door to a quest for
Liberation which I'm still pursuing

And Jim is a big fellow with skillful
Woodworking hands and a cheerful and a
Gentle comportment and a twinkle in
His eyes reflecting a secret which is

Always open to anyone lucky
Enough to have stumbled upon the path.

Jim and I agree
that there are many
American Zen
priests but very few
genuine masters.

There is a world beyond my thoughts where things
Happen spontaneously in every
Direction ceaselessly and I would love
To be in harmony without the weight

Of the burden of my thoughts and I am
Bound with worries and cravings and sometimes
I'm awake hours before the dawn and
I realize that I am clouding the

World with the impetus of my worries
And cravings and I haven't discovered
The way to liberation yet but at
Least I do have a clue about the

Nature of my troubles and having a
Companion like Jim is very helpful.

The *Dharma* is transmitted
from person to person
and a liberated
personality is
key.

Jim is still doing all of the things he
Used to do three decades ago such as
Japanese calligraphy and drawing
Kanji with his horsehair brushes with a

Flourish of his wrist and hand and to
Me the letters look like blotches of ink
On paper but to Jim they are forms that
Rise up in three dimensions and he sees

The flowing dance of the brush as if in
Imitation of the graceful verve
Of a *katana* slicing through the air
And there are very few people with the

Discernment to appreciate the pith
Of the motion — but Jim keeps doing it.

Jim's happy to do
repeatedly over the
decades an art that
is unappreciated
because he's still improving.

Jim's gentle and baritone words brought back
To me the memories that I could have
Gained in no other way as I relish
Being a companion on Jim's journey

Gleaning through his eyes the ambience of
The San Francisco Zen Center and his
Acquaintance with its founding Zen master
Shunryu Suzuki who upended his

Students by breaking cherished traditions
In one case tricking an earnest novice
Into eating a hamburger using
Humor and intelligence to make an

Unforgettable point driving home a
Ploy of spontaneous innovation.

Using traditions by
upsetting the traditions
effectively and
humorously is a ploy
of a liberated guy.

Kitcat is perilous like a tiger
He doesn't care that he's only pint size
Extending no more than a foot lengthwise
I know him to be a ready biter
With the inclination of a fighter
He stares ferociously with tiger's eyes
With an intensity to hypnotize
Taut and tense in every nervy fiber
While he knows my habits — and I know his
I sing him tunes of nonsense quality
He flops on the floor and shows his belly
Does he want to play? He certainly does
He's quite capable of frivolity
And I know his belly feels like jelly.

He has the ferocity
Along with sinuosity
Pouncing with pleasure
He's very clever
But he lacks verbosity.

I've not been one to follow conventions
Instead I've taken odd romantic jobs
Shorn of the dignity preferred by snobs
I know I cherish certain pretensions
That come with a load of expectations
One can't seek clarity and be a slob
Or cater to the whims of vicious mobs
I want to be clear in my intentions
And to play with words and make a living
Forgoing a rewarding salary
To linger with the inexpressible
To play with notions of awakening
Though my method may be a fallacy
I do aim to be comprehensible.

It may not be credible
Or even respectable
To try to profit
By writing sonnets
But it is delectable.

I do understand your emotions and
Know that you're having a difficult time
And seeking for balance in the meantime
Letting go of a marriage that has spanned
Maybe three decades and that you can't stand
Being dispensed with when you're in your prime
Which indicates a ton of loss and I'm
Not disoriented and am on hand
To divert the agitation of your
Thoughts with the exploration of my words
As there's no need to be stuck in the past
When you could be hopeful and open doors
And as I am you could be looking toward
A liberation and a peace that lasts.

Driving around to
bars to see whether his car
is parked outside
isn't fun and I'd rather
do anything else with you.

I get a boost talking to you every
Morning on the phone when most people are
Still sleeping in bed and it is bizarre
That we can be exchanging repartee
Consuming an hour in reverie
So who would care to get drunk in a bar
Or to be constantly picking at scars
And be writhing about in dependency
When intimacy alleviates so
Much of our compulsive agitation
And there's no substitute for feeling loved
Which I missed through years of living solo
And now that's ending with conversation
As you're making me feel understood.

Some days I wake up
early and count the minutes
until I can call
and hear again your cheerful
voice I am accustomed to.

The American soldier is so poorly
Appreciated by Americans
Who don't care much about Afghanistan
While soldiers take honor seriously
And they dedicate their lives to duty
As they follow orders and garrison
The most belligerent and distant land
Not questioning the nation's policy
But America suffers poor leadership
So blame the presidents and generals
And our governing class is terrible
Lost in petty venal partisanship
Where the blame-shifting is perennial
And their constant lies are contemptible.

The burden of our
nation's mistakes falls upon
honor-bound soldiers
and their families while the
elites appropriate wealth.

Arrogance and incompetence are on
The rise in American leadership
Coming with deceiving partisanship
In a news media that strings along
Narratives designed not only to con
Americans but also to equip
Politicians with propaganda stripped
Of heartfelt regard for the truth forgone
Because our intellectuals are more
Interested in power and control
And now Americans are bitterly
Divided which is harder to ignore
As every calamity takes a toll
And politicians fail repeatedly.

Righteous
propaganda
inspires
fellow-feeling in
everyone except
its targets.

I am a droplet of the universe
And I embody its propensities
For dissolution and ascendency
And I do determine the impetus
Of direction from the secret impulse
Of my thoughts that pivot incessantly
In a delicate dance tentatively
Balanced between the better and the worse
And I need to be aware when the tenor
Of my thinking is mostly negative
And I'm soliciting unhappiness
And then it helps very much to explore
The releasing of thoughts generative
Of a welcome relaxation and peace.

Circumstances do
impose leverage over
times but a watchful
and persisting gentleness
emboldens optimism.

I traveled to Ohio to visit
Relatives and to take my elderly
Mother to meet her sister tenderly
Reuniting the two from the limits
Of distance and time making explicit
All the buried memories heartily
At a surprise party sprung cheerfully
On my mother's sister and we did it
To celebrate her sister's 90th
Birthday and the sisters will have very
Much to talk and to reminisce over
And the moment of meeting took my breath
Watching their reunion became teary
With a wealth of liveliness left over.

Beloved husbands
children
grandchildren
great-grandchildren
the vanishing world —
so much to discuss.

The fingers and ankles and the balls of
The feet are vital components of a
Bicycle rider as I learned with the
Use of a light carbon fiber bike of
Superior quality with the shoes of
A different clip-on style and with the
Gear shifting mechanism needing a
Challenging and puzzling sequence of
Finger manipulation new to me
Which I had to remember on the fly
And my ankles are attuned to the twist
That frees the shoe from the pedal but I
Couldn't click into the pedal and missed
Much too often as I strove to apply
Directional pressure to get the gist.

My brother loaned me
the use of his best bike which
unexpectedly
demanded a different
display of dexterity.

I am a simple guy with a speedy
Aluminum bicycle at home but
My brother drives to distant trails and puts
His bikes on a rack on a luxury
Car and he can track his proximity
Heart rate and wind speed and I don't know what
Else but besides all that he has the guts
To ride like he's crazy repeatedly
Over the years and I was proud to keep
Up and surprised that I could fixing my
Attention on him because suddenly
He'd race and the rivers and trees would sweep
By but after several good hours I
Did get tired and moved exhaustedly.

Days later he sent
me an email with graphs of
elevation with
exact locations and a
sum of our average speed.

I am reading an Agatha Christie
Murder mystery about what appeared to
Be a double suicide having to
Do with a respectable and happy
Couple of British high society
Which occurred a decade previous to
The events of the story which turned to
An examination of memory
Involving insights gleaned from the British
Empire giving weight to the phrase that
"An elephant remembers" implying
That telling clues however diminished
Lie dormant within incomplete views that
Disparate people hold that need sifting.

Like the elephants
people cherish opinions
precariously
based on uncertain facts that
are disappearing targets.

The furrowed brow and comprehending eyes
Of elephants are curious clues to
A sensibility with a strange view
That implies that they surely could be wise
To predicaments and choices with ties
Of volatility of what to do
Within the circumstances leading to
Their haphazard impulses when surprised
And if the expression is true that the
Elephants remember the insults or
The generosity of people from
Years ago then they are truly due a
Sympathetic respect and a rapport
Earned from the mystery from which we come.

If I were born with
the trunk the enormous girth
the feet and the ears
of an elephant I would
cavort with lumbering strength.

It's better to admit that it's bigger
Than you and over time it will beat you
Down and will thoroughly discourage you
And you've heard enough lies to be bitter
And you do yourself damage to bicker
And after the divorce it's clear you're through
So what is it that you're trying to do?
As you know he's not a normal drinker
And an alcoholic won't get better
And if he's not willing to save himself
You know there is nothing that you can do
You're divorced — it's done — so be a quitter
It's way past time to take care of yourself —
I've reached a limit of what I can do.

You've got to admit
that you've hit a wall with him
there's nothing to do
other than to let him deal
with his alcoholism.

There is a way to get out of trouble
Whether a person is alcoholic
Or is one who loves an alcoholic
And it really is inevitable
And after it's done it's not a puzzle
You've got to admit that the guy is sick
And then surrendering becomes the trick
Then finally things are manageable
There just *has* to be an end to fighting
When every effort to control it flops
The only answer is relaxation
I know even though he might be dying
Your intention to cure it has to stop —
Try to let go of your expectations.

When I finally
admitted that I was an
alcoholic a
weight was lifted from my
shoulders and I became free.

She says — I went over to his house the
Very home where we raised our family
And I saw the mess of his apathy —
The counter was cluttered with dishes — the
Carpet was dirty — things were scattered — the
Dog was tense and ready to bite me —
There was a sense of unreality
With him sitting on the stairs and in a
Daze in his underwear before he had
To dress for work and seeing him like that
I thought he's not attractive anymore
And I couldn't be mad but sure was sad
To see the misery he's arrived at
With our history which I can't ignore.

And now I don't have
to be thinking about him
any more and I
can be free from whatever
compulsive needs I had.

I say that — I try to remember when
I'm sad or unhappy for whatever
Reason or when I'm feeling the pressure
Of being separate from people in
My life that the Eastern *Dharma* begins
With suffering and that I will suffer
Because of my stubbornness whenever
I can't let go of something but I can
Remember and see the simplicity
Of the point that if I'm not clinging to
What I want then I won't be suffering
But I admit I have difficulty
Doing my best at letting go — and to
Be better at that I am practicing.

Doing my best while
letting go of results is
a propitious
trick of relaxation that
I haven't begun to master.

I can't practice very well on my own
And I need people who share at least some
Of the ideas I'm using who can come
To understanding me and to be shown
How better it is than being alone
And I think you know where I'm coming from
And I'm telling you that it means a ton
To be listening to you on the phone
As we both know from experience that
Alcoholism is deadly and there's
So much more to be had from life than to
Be isolated and lonely in what
Is certain to become a mess that spares
No misery — not knowing what to do.

If what I say sounds
crazy imagine how things
would be if I had
no one to mitigate the
nonsense inside of my head.

I catch myself at odd moments saying
To myself when nobody but me is
Listening that "she is my girl" and is
This really true as I am suspecting
That my subconsciousness is asserting
That "she is my girl" and in fact she does
Love me and in idle moments she does
Care for me as much as I am caring
About her? But perhaps it's true that by force
Of will I am repeating a guess that
I desperately hope to be the truth
When I know deep down that I can't enforce
My wishes on reality and that
I may be fooling myself with half-truths.

I do have to watch
such messages when part of
me is trying to
convince the other part they're
true — when they may not be true.

There was the nagging incident when I
Waited at a restaurant for 40
Minutes alone for her and she hardly
Expressed a reason and as a nice guy
I didn't quibble wanting to get by
Without unpleasantness — and again we
Were at a restaurant being carefree
Having a good time when things went awry
When she saw a man she knew before and
Invited him to join us unmindful
Of my feelings and the two of them were
Eagerly engaged excluding me and
I do admit that I was resentful
Lonely frustrated and doubtful of her.

Another time she
spoke to a waiter about
me in a manner
that wasn't quite respectful
as I sat by stoically.

When we meet together in public there
Is a good chance that we'll have fun and that
I'll drive home satisfied and thinking that
The night couldn't have gone better aware
Of emotional burdens that she bears
But sometimes it's true that I'm feeling flat
With worries that I don't want to look at
With nagging suspicions it may be fair
To question her regard for me and yet
When we speak on the phone before the dawn
Every day I am able to express
My heartfelt words and then I do forget
My doubts because of the joy I live on
Because conversation feels like success.

The facility
of expression that we share
in morning hours
has in it for me the joy
of being comprehended.

A spasm of the neck afflicted her
When she was alone in her living room
Which was a sharp searing pain I assume
While I was on my bike and nowhere near
And perhaps it felt like a sudden tear
And afterwards there was persisting gloom
Which she felt in the emergency room
As being old isn't easy for her
And so I was called to the hospital
I noticed she was well attended to
But my mother was weary and confused
She isn't moving well and she's brittle
So we have a course of treatment to do
And another stage of life is opened.

There were episodes
in the past with spasms in
her back that she's been
able to overcome so
there's reason to be hopeful.

I've noticed it and perhaps you have too
That dust accumulates inside a house
It would be helpful to have a loving spouse
There is so much maintenance to do
With little nagging chores to get through
And I have no remedy to espouse
No easy revelation to announce
There are some adjustments to attend to
When one of a married couple dies first
There was the joy of many loving years
Looked back upon with appreciation
Then suddenly that time of life is burst
And we are presented with strange new cares
Can we make a reevaluation?

My mom was always
the quiet underlying
security of our
family cooking suppers
and civilizing her kids.

I had an idea — but forgot it
I had it — but I'm not remembering
Now I'm stuck and sitting here questioning
Sometimes I suspect I'm losing my wits
Perhaps by now I'm only a half-wit
I was in the habit of note-taking
Reading a note is reawakening
But I've been lazy and not doing it —
You see it's so important to be on
The lookout for the spark of insight that
Springs a poem and when it comes I need to
Recognize it appreciate it on
The spot and seize on the catalyst that
Makes possible all the hullabaloo.

It's like entering
a room and realizing
you have forgotten
why you came — inspiration
slips quickly through my fingers.

Agatha Christie is an expert at
Revealing a person's character with
A quirk of speech in her dialogues with
A spice of intriguing happenings that
Impels me to keep reading even at
A time of night when I'd be sleeping with
My dreams as she is a maestro wordsmith
Who makes me jealous dangling her clues that
May amount to nothing or not but there
Are too many clues mixed with the details
Of plot to keep track of and I truly
Love her depiction of the British where
Subtle class distinctions make for blackmail
Within the rank of high society.

She reveals the
weakness and the meanness in
the disorder of
human nature directing
motivation to murder.

Agatha Christie clued me into the
Fact that I am a "dipsomaniac"
Which is a word meaning alcoholic
Which says I'm a "dipso" added to a
"Mania" which means I could be a
"Maniac" which is quite a verbal whack
Which implies people like me need smacks
To keep us soberly sensible in a
 World that expects much better of us
And I'm not going to quibble about that
As we have maniacal qualities
But I am not a dilophosaurus
Which was a toothy dinosaur that
Had much worse antisocial qualities.

Agatha Christie
uses her verbosity
quite responsibly
and she only had to use
the word once to make her point.

My house which I have almost finished paying
For is looking a little worse for wear and
The joints between my pipes are leaky and
I've put up with it for a while thinking
That my iron pipes will be expanding
Because colder weather is coming and
Isn't that what iron does when cold and
I saw how stupid I was admitting
I had to call a plumber reluctantly
Because I'm stingy but I did make the call
For a plumber and he said that pipes will
Leak and then he got to work and quickly
Discovered that a rubber hose had caused all
The mess which he fixed and gave me a bill.

I am a wordy
intellectual who could
convince himself that
iron pipes will expand in
cold and therefore stop the leaks.

I received an email today about
The Sistine Chapel which included a
Virtual tour which presented me a
Panoramic view and I could check out
The exquisite designs and expand out
The smallest details with a flick of the
Wrist and with a shift of the mouse of a
Mac computer which is nothing to pout
About and the email informed me that
Pope Julius became impatient with
Michelangelo because he believed
The artist was too dilatory at
The job and so the Pope questioned him with
Pique: Why was he so slow at what he did?

Michelangelo
answered Pope Julius
by saying that he
was still learning —
"Ancora Imparo."

Now we have entered into September
Which does make me somewhat melancholy
I'm a little sad — but not unhappy
As I'm at an age when I remember
All the many times we've turned this corner
Maybe I am prematurely sappy
A little somber — though not unhappy
This isn't the darkness of December
There will be plenty of warm days to come
I'll ride my bike as often as I can
And savor every change of the season
By watching the quality of the sun
And noticing its diminishing span
As summer is reaching its completion.

The glare of the sun
is diminishing in the
evening and the light
touching my cottonwood leaves
has a golden glow about it.

In the affairs of state involving the
Conduct of warfare and of strategy
It's painful to perceive complacency
And negligence in the betters of a
Republic who wouldn't when they had the
Time order their plans with competency
So at the point of crisis they betray
Citizens and faithful allies and the
Families of our warriors even
In the event surrendering people
Into the clutches of the enemy
Unto death whatever one believes in
When our leaders lie it's contemptible
To covet power without decency.

Thousands of faithful
allies and American
citizens were left
behind in Afghanistan
by America's betters.

The dwelling where my family lived for
Most of my childhood is on the north hill
Of Stillwater and so the rooms are filled
With memories almost forgotten or
Over the verge of consciousness stored
Latently somehow within me but still
Available being bygone until
A turn of my thinking opens a door
For instance when I notice an object
Among hundreds of other objects that
Returns to present awareness a tang
Of emotional insight that connects
Whomever I was with who I am that
Delivers to me a walloping pang.

The oak rocking chair
In the living room where my Dad
used to watch football
on Sunday afternoons has
comfortable resonance.

My mom suffered a spasm of her neck
And now she can't turn her head to the left
She needs looking after and so I check
Whether she is eating and getting rest
The doctor prescribed her several pills
She needs reminding of when to take them
The pain in her head is making her ill
She's not defeated — just a little glum
But I am noticing that she's forgetful
She can't recall what happened yesterday
She eats so little that I get fretful
When I push her to eat she does give way
To get better she needs some directions
She doesn't have so many objections.

When awake she stays
bent over on the couch with
a hot or cold pack
pressed upon her neck as the
doctor has directed her.

The clouds are drifting to the south today
And the sky is filled with warm gentle light
And there was a hurricane yesterday
But not a hint of that in this sunlight
Much of America was torn by storm
So many houses were struck and destroyed
I do forget that such storms are the norm
And that tragedies are hard to avoid
The leaves today are suffused with the light
The glow of sun is blissfully peaceful
The turn toward autumn is beautifully bright
I have no reason to be regretful
The trouble is over the horizon
In the south it is hurricane season.

I would much rather
suffer the impending cold
and the blizzards of
Minnesota than the news
of another hurricane
brewing off of the Gulf Coast.

I've been noticing the patterns of birds
I saw a flock of sparrows yesterday
How can I capture them only with words?
We heard a boisterous blue jay today
The jay interrupted a Zoom meeting
And we absorbed it on a microphone
Most of my views of birds are fleeting
I see them flying between trees alone
Some days ago I saw a chickadee
On my bicycle I spotted a gull
There are turkey vultures in twos and threes
I don't believe I've heard a vulture's call
So many birds will be migrating soon
They will be returning again in June.

Toucans flamingos
Galápagos penguins and
various parrots
are birds that never venture
to frozen Minnesota.

She's wearing a bright yellow summer dress
With a string top exposing her shoulders
It's apparent she's dressing to impress
Stimulating an urge to embrace her
I'm guessing excitement can be helpful
Prompting me to be alert and fluent
To play with my words — and to be cheerful
I'm even able to experiment
To venture a little pleasing teasing
Hinting at her availability
Expressing that she's very appealing
That she could well be another Sherry
In response she's very animated
This is better than anticipated.

The Kung Pao Chicken
with spicy chili sauce and
with green onions and
with red chili peppers went
by without much noticing.

Sherry is a woman who works with her
Sherry teases guys and gets rid of them
She is not like Sherry but if she were
I'd never be beneath anyone's thumb
I love the conversation and banter
Tonight we shared devoted attention
She didn't make remarks to the waiter
There were no moments of apprehension
She's very savvy and stimulating
And does make me feel appreciated
Sometimes she can be almost insulting
And I don't like being disrespected
I will play along with her for a while
More often than not she's making me smile.

I am thinking how
much easier it would be
not to be thought of
as having to call her and
entertain her so often.

I parked my Corolla along the edge
Of the parking lot lengthwise because the
Places in the middle were taken and
I did have misgivings but I ignored

Them and when the meeting finished and I
Returned to my car I was surprised by
An apologetic young woman who
Confessed to backing into my car and

We examined a slight dent disrupting
The stylish aerodynamic angles
Of my driver's side rear passenger door
And I didn't call the police to make

A report because she waited for me
And I trusted she would do the right thing.

She didn't return
my calls and thus refused to
cooperate with
the insurance claim so the
dent will be decorative.

The sky to the south overlooking the
River valley is full of the morning
Light gentle and warm and let it be a
Replacement of my thoughts as the geese are

Spanning the expanse in an elegant
Line of flight and I don't know where they are
Going and the sprinklers in the park have
Stopped and drops of water are speckling a

A steel park bench and refracting the light
With rainbow brilliance and three crows chase each
Other past the maple tree intent on
Some kind of competition and the oak

Spreads its green leaves unmindful of the change
Of the seasons poised and prospering now.

I listen to my
sober dipsomaniacs
and speak in my turn
but I am also inside
the phantasmagoria.

I used Agatha Christie by reading
Her novel up until the moment I
Went to bed happily yesterday at
The point when the murder was announced and

Every character is smoldering with
Hidden motivations and there's a fog
Of puzzling ambience to chew over
Which fascinates me and allows me to

Forget about myself so that chances
Are I won't wake up at 3 a.m. with
Enough nervous energy to prevent
Me from sleeping and even if I wake

I can dwell on the labors of Hercule
Poirot or on Jane Marple's cleverness.

The mayhem of an
Agatha Christie novel
is preferable
to the moroseness of my
3 a.m. meditations.

I can put the words on this paper that
Contain the meaning of the emptiness
Of things that propose that there is no birth
And no death and also no being and

No nonbeing and that there can be no
Defilement when there is no purity
And that along with the body there is
Emptiness and that the body is not

Different from emptiness but is in
Fact the same as emptiness and there are
No eyes and ears and nose and tongue and skin
No sight and sound and smell and taste and touch

And the meanings of these words imply these
Words are nonsensically meaningless.

Yet for some reason
for thousands of years people
have taken these words
to heart and a few of them
profess realization.

On this particular piece of paper
Bound together with other pages on
The left and surrounded by margins there
Are words arranged into orderly lines

Wherein letters are stuck to each other
That compose syllables which may be read
Silently or spoken out loud and the
Combined meaning flows along from the left

To the right and you may read up or down
Or right to left and obtain gibberish
Or you may follow convention to get
The gist of the meaning and thus achieve

Comprehension and in conclusion you
May decide if the trip was worth taking.

After the trip the
import of the words lingers
for a moment but
eventually they will
dissolve into emptiness.

Seeing school buses going by on the
Streets again after the summer break is
Over brings back memories of concerns
Lasting over decades whether my kids

Were learning measuring up and getting
Along mixing with the others of their
Age as they were already laying down
The patterns of their lives being lonely

Hurt and disappointed along with their
Successes while I questioned if I was
Doing enough and where would the money
To pay for college come from which was a

Hurdle I didn't dwell on much but I
Guessed we'd find a way to graduation.

They are
intelligent
educated
graduated
engaged in life
and out of the house.

I am stubborn and don't want to close the
Windows of my house even though the air
Before dawn when I wake and move about
Is becoming more than cool and verging

Into chilly and I gave up going
Barefoot and acquiesced to wearing socks
Inside slippers and I put on my long
Pants and long sleeves and I am accustomed

Now to the preponderance of darkness
Extending further into the morning
As I fold into the lotus posture
And notice the absence of birdsong and

The percolation of coffee and the
Dog barking at a point in the distance.

I am not ready
yet to give in and to close
the windows and then
to resort to the furnace
and thus to be hunkered down.

The link on the Internet that gives me a
A panoramic and intimate view
Of the Sistine Chapel and lets me see
The twelve high windows through which the light shines

Helped me to picture Michelangelo
On a scaffold standing and reaching up
Awkwardly to the ceiling as he took
The drops of paint that speckled his face for

The four long years of his labor and how
Important those windows must have been to
Let in the daylight illuminating
And clarifying what he had done and

How much further there was to go in the
Creation of his view of Creation.

Michelangelo
lived without the blessing of
electricity
confined within the borders
of vivid darkness and light.

I see it in the air in September
Before the bulk of the leaves begin to
Flower into autumn colors as the
Shadows lengthen in the twilight of the

Morning and evening and the haze that's so
Typical of summer afternoons cleared
And is replaced by a crispness and when
I ride my bicycle the heat is not

Present and the glare of the sun does not
Bleach the color from the trees but instead
The lustrous leaves are tinged with the yellow
Of the sun and there is quiet and it

Is cool and the sun in the open sky
Retains its brilliance but is past its peak.

We had rainy days
and the fields of corn have grown
tall and the grass is
green and growing but there is
a conclusion in the air.

Decisions have to be made as my Mom
Is forgetting whether she took all of
Her pills and she can't remember when to
Take them and I'm not there enough to keep

Track and after her neck spasm her head
Continuously aches and she told my
Sister a different story about
The nature of her accident than she

Told me involving a fall that I was
Unaware of and it's tricky to know
Whether she's eating and drinking enough
To sustain herself and she's sleeping and

I don't want to disturb her yet but I
Do need to get her to the clinic soon.

Relaxed
and poised

is the best
I can do

waiting for
inspiration.

Mom is an accumulator of stuff
And her house is tidy and organized
And every drawer and closet is full
Of things that were put there decades ago

And we children have always known the days will
Come when the sanctuary of comfort
That my mother has woven will have to
Be undone and the weightiness and the grief

Involved with the task is a dread that we
Contain in an out-of-the-way drawer
In our minds but now events are moving
Beyond control with debate arising

Among we siblings over whether she
Is able to be safe inside her home.

I'm getting ahold
of what medicine she needs
at what times and I'm
seeing that she's eating
so order is emerging.

I need to know what and whom I can trust
And I sincerely put faith in people
Until they show me by their behavior
Without question they are untrustworthy

Then I let go of my expectations
Which takes painful practice but I do trust
That when I fold my body into the
Lotus position and meditate that

I will escape for a time the realm of
Human hysteria by attending
To the radical simplicity of
My breath and the beating of my heart which

Remind me that I am only a
Droplet within a cosmic consciousness.

It's manageable
by noticing my breath and
my beating heart to
quell my racing thoughts and to
dwell within simplicity.

A memory of this porch lives in me
Of when it was newly built of lovely
Wood panels and the foldout bed is here
Where Yoshiko and I slept while we were

On vacation in America and
It was the first time for my Japanese
Wife to visit the country and I was
Looking at my hometown and the house where

I grew up and also my Mom and Dad
With fresh appreciative eyes after
Living abroad for several years and now
I'm divorced my Dad has passed and my Mom

Is frail but the optimism of the
Time 30 years ago lives sadly on.

The huge cottonwood
under which I mowed the lawn
as a teenager
was cut down because of
the strike of a lightning bolt.

"I worry . . ." she says as if it were a
Badge of honor and she can't because she's
Busy but something needs doing and so
She recommends that I rush Mom to the

Clinic to have Dr. Wessel check the
Bump on her neck to consider if
A biopsy is necessary as
I hear barely suppressed hysteria

Inside her voice and I do acknowledge
The sincerity and the assistance
My sister's given in looking after
Mom but I do regret her habit of

Running in frenzied circles and then her
Insistence that I run in circles too.

Impassively I
listen imitating as
well as I might
the Rock of Gibraltar as
I refuse to be frazzled.

P.S. There is no bump.

**Things that Happened
At the Poetry Workshop**

- A guy strode determinedly by in a
Gray- and white-striped T shirt and red sneakers
- A woman nearby erupted in a
Vituperate rage about something
- A guy by a trailer was lazily
Putting branches into a woodchipper
- The East Side Freedom Library built by
Andrew Carnegie was quite imposing
- The leaves made a lovely shade for us as
We sat in lawn chairs circled on the grass
- A window washer leisurely plied a
Long-handled squeegee to the church windows
- I thoroughly enjoyed the relaxing
Ambience of a Saturday morning.

In between each of
the above we read out loud
and silently each
other's poems and then we
traded our commentary.

What I like about writing poetry
Is that I can eliminate so much
Of the clutter in my life by simply
Not including it inside of the words

That I choose to put on paper even
Though it is there fighting for my precious
Attention and energy but instead
I may focus on optimism and

Panache and compose lines of crystalline
Meaning without ambiguity as
I don't demand that my readers perform
Cerebral acrobatics to achieve

Comprehension and I smile picturing
The smile I put on my readers' faces.

Half of the mission
of a life should be to squeeze
frivolity from
conundrums along with the
humdrum preoccupations.

By the time we get to the hind part of
A book of poetry I imagine
You my readers are perhaps a little
Impatient to finish and be done with

Me because I'm like that too even with
Agatha Christie who is as fine a
Writer as could be wished for but may I
Encumber you with a modest pointer?

That the rhymed sonnets are intricate and
Subtle and may be read enjoyably
Over again as there is a game of
Rhyming odd words and half-rhyming going

On that perhaps escaped your notice on
The first harried dashing through the pages.

My unrhymed sonnets
are trifling and frivolous
composed amid the
hurly burly and hysteria
with a gesture of castoff ease.

So simple is William Wordsworth's poem
Of a violet "among untrodden
Ways" hidden by a "mossy stone" and so
Apropos to the "maid" Lucy who

Lived with "very few to love" or "to praise
Her" or to know when "she ceased to be" but
To William Lucy was as "Fair as a
Star" and William uses just a few words

As fitting as an epitaph on a
Gravestone to memorialize his love
And I had quite forgotten his little
Poem until happenstance returned it

To me and I suggest you read it too
In honor of William and of Lucy.

May William and Lucy
be a perennial
memory of a
memory.

Twenty years ago on Tuesday morning
Two highjacked airliners flew into the
World Trade Center and then in a scene of
Horror the two massive towers fell and

Filled the open sky with billowing clouds
Of toxic dust and debris and while the
Heroes of the day the firemen and
Police are as resolute as ever

And America's soldiers are battle-
Scarred and are as disciplined as ever
America's leaders are proving to be
Both arrogant and incompetent and

Unworthy of the sacrifice of those
Who have died in America's defense.

There is bitterness
and ruination in the
affairs of state and
no end to the suffering
of ordinary people.

Among the green leaves
a breeze drops but
a few yellow leaves
keep falling.

—*Tekkan*

www.ingramcontent.com/pod-product-compliance
Lightning Source LLC
Chambersburg PA
CBHW040107120526
44589CB00039B/2786